STINKY ABCs

Written by Debra J. Mines

Pictures by Henry M. Blackmon III

STINKY SHOES Series

Copyright © 2022 Author: Debra J. Mines

Illustrator: Henry M. Blackmon III

All rights reserved. This book is protected under the copyright laws of the United States of America. Any reproduction or other unauthorized use of any part of this book by any means, graphic, electronic, photocopying, recording, taping or by any information storage retrieval system is prohibited without the written permission of the author.

Kindle Direct Publishing
https://kdp.amazon.com

Table of Contents

iii	**FOREWORD**
v	**SPECIAL THANKS and DEDICATION**
1	**ABCs**
32	**READ *STINKY ABCs* ALL OVER AGAIN**
33	**ACTIVITY 1: VOCABULARY**
34	**WORD BANK**
35	**ACTIVITY 1**
61	**ANSWER KEY for ACTIVITY 1**
64	**ACTIVITY 2: PRACTICE**
67	**ANSWER KEY for ACTIVITY 2**
70	**ABOUT THE AUTHOR**

Foreword

The author, Debra J. Mines, wrote *STINKY ABCs* after much reflection on the features that an ideal alphabet book should present to young children.

Debra J. Mines remembers searching through numerous libraries and bookstores for the best ABC books to teach her firstborn, a baby girl, how to read and later to teach her baby boy how to read, as well. The ideal alphabet books were difficult to find because very few of them contained large, distinguishable upper-case and lower-case letters with clear, captivating pictures to match the letters.

Remembering this experience motivated Debra J. Mines to design **STINKY ABCs**.

Enjoy Reading!

Special Thanks

Beverly London receives special thanks for being a caring and supportive sister during the writing of *STINKY ABCs*.

Dedication

This book is dedicated to my daughter, Hermalena V. Mines Powell, and my son, Clifford H. Mines, for becoming avid readers despite my many trials while searching for the perfect alphabet book.

Phew-oo-oo-oo-wee!

A a is for stinky, aging apples.

B b *is for stinky, babbling bananas.*

C c is for stinky,

choppy cantaloupes.

E e is for stinky, eagle's eggs.

F f is for stinky, fidgety feet.

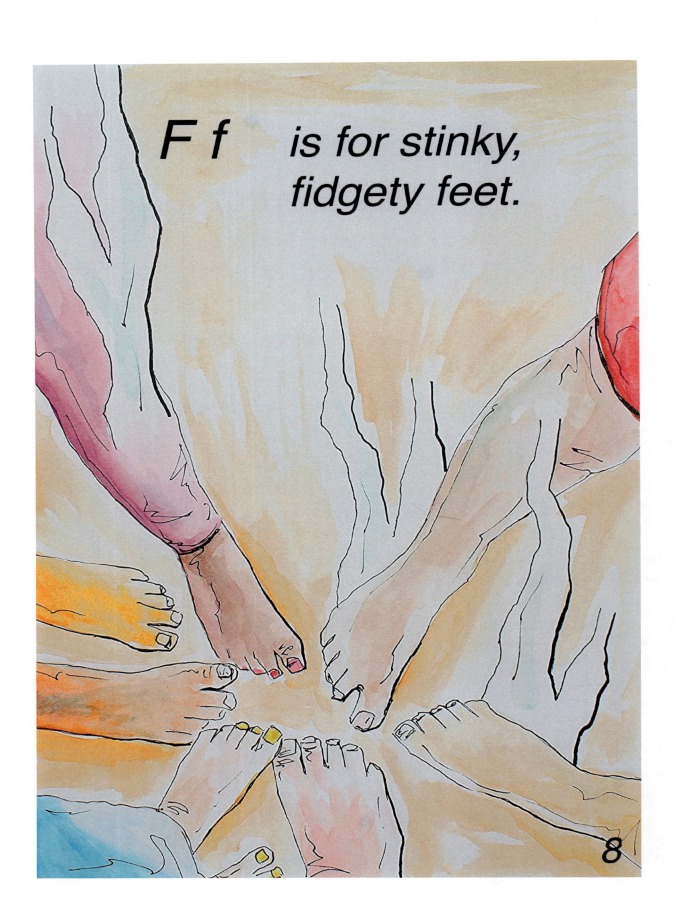

G g
is for stinky, galloping galoshes.

H h is for stinky, huge houseflies.

I i *is for stinky, icky iguanas.*

J j
is for
stinky,

jumping

jeans!

12

K k is for stinky, king-size keyboards.

L l is for stinky, lazy lizards.

M m

is for

stinky, muddy monkeys.

N n is for stinky number 9.

O o is for stinky, outrageous orangutans.

P p
is for stinky,

pigheaded pigs.

Q q is for stinky, quiet quails.

R r is for stinky, racing raccoons.

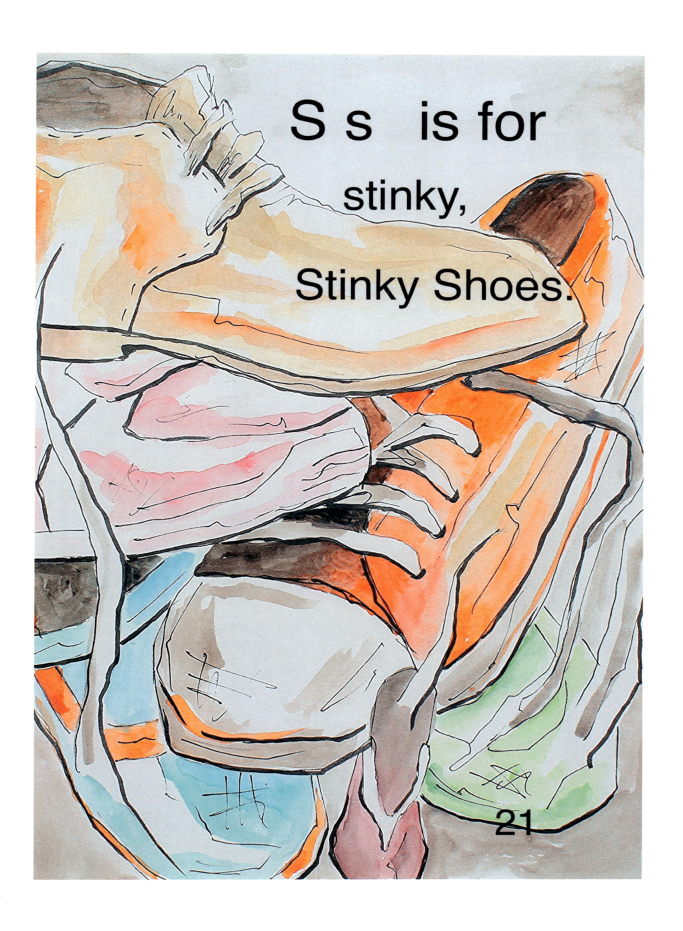

S s is for stinky, Stinky Shoes.

T t is for stinky, terrible tarantulas.

U u is for stinky, ugly umbrellas.

W w is for stinky, wiggly worms.

X x is for stinky, Xylo xylophones.

Y y is for stinky, yawning yaks.

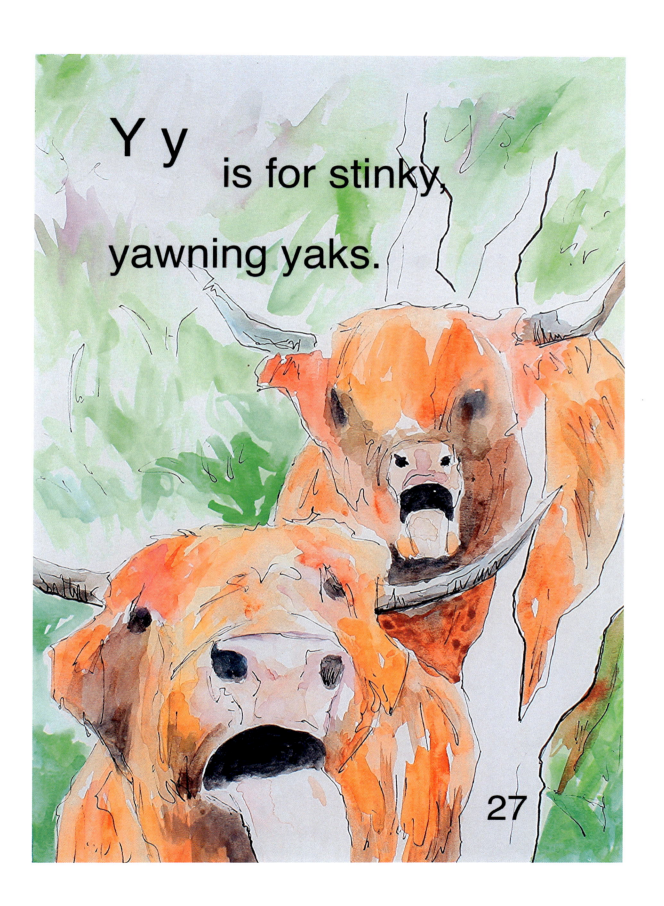

Z z is for stinky, zippy zebras.

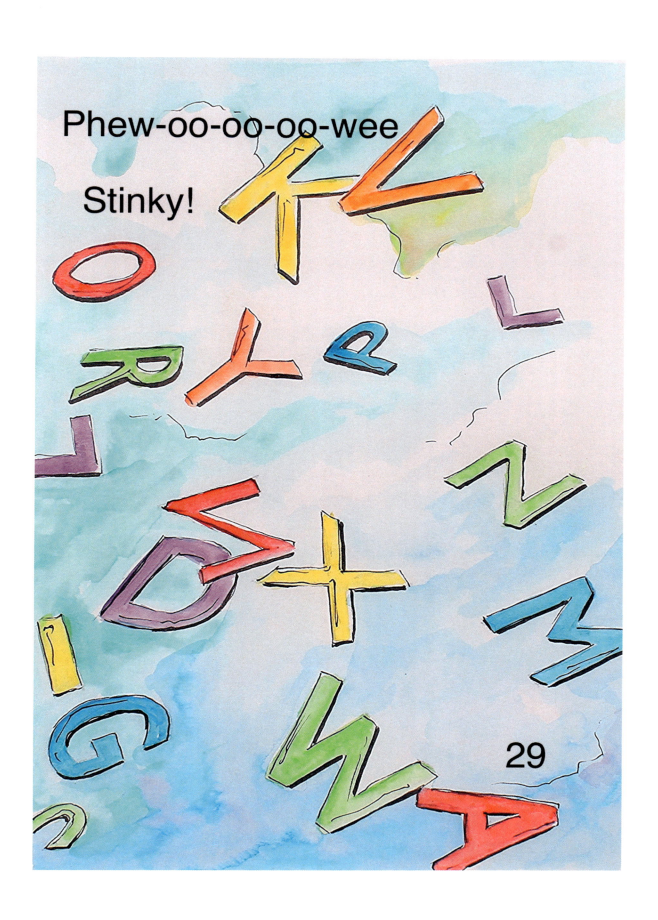

Phew-oo-oo-oo-wee

Stinky!

OH-H-H NO!

Read *Stinky ABCs*

all over again!

Activity 1: Vocabulary

Directions:

1. Look at the word bank on page 34.
2. Choose words from the word bank to fill in the blank lines for each letter of the alphabet on pages 35 – 60.
3. Draw a picture for each letter of the alphabet on pages 35 – 60.

Word Bank

babbling bananas	dirty dogs
terrible tarantulas	ugly umbrellas
galloping galoshes	wiggly worms
muddy monkeys	fidgety feet
quiet quails	vacant vans
Xylo xylophones	number nine
Stinky Shoes	yawning yaks
king-size keyboards	aging apples
choppy cantaloupes	lazy lizards
eagle's eggs	zippy zebras
huge houseflies	icky Iguanas
jumping jeans	racing raccoons
pig-headed pigs	orange orangutans

Activity 1

Aa   is for stinky,

_____.

Picture Box

Bb   is for stinky,

_____.

Picture Box

Cc is for stinky,

_____.

Picture Box

Dd is for stinky,

_____.

Picture Box

Ee   is for stinky,

_____.

Picture Box

Ff is for stinky,

_____.

Picture Box

Gg   is for stinky,

_____.

Picture Box

Hh is for stinky,

_____.

Picture Box

Ii is for stinky,

_____.

Picture Box

Jj is for stinky,

_____.

Picture Box

Kk is for stinky,

_____.

Picture Box

Ll is for stinky,

_____.

Picture Box

Mm   is for stinky,

_____.

Picture Box

Nn is for stinky,

_____.

Picture Box

Oo   is for stinky,

_____.

Picture Box

Pp   is for stinky,

_____.

Picture Box

Qq is for stinky,

_____.

Picture Box

Rr is for stinky,

_____.

Picture Box

Ss is for stinky,

_____.

Picture Box

Tt is for stinky,

_____.

Picture Box

Uu is for stinky,

_____.

Picture Box

Vv   is for stinky,

_____.

Picture Box

Ww is for stinky,

_____.

Picture Box

Xx   is for stinky,

_____.

Picture Box

Yy is for stinky,

_____.

Picture Box

Zz is for stinky,

_____.

Picture Box

Answer Key for Activity 1

Aa   is for stinky, aging apples.

Bb   is for stinky, babbling bananas.

Cc   is for stinky, choppy cantaloupes.

Dd   is for stinky, dirty dogs.

Ee   is for stinky, eagle's eggs.

Ff   is for stinky, fidgety feet.

Gg   is for stinky, galloping galoshes.

Hh   is for stinky, huge houseflies.

Ii   is for stinky, icky iguanas.

Jj is for stinky, jumping jeans.

Kk is for stinky, king-size keyboards.

Ll is for stinky, lazy lizards.

Mm is for stinky, muddy monkeys.

Nn is for stinky number nine.

Oo is for stinky, orange orangutans.

Pp is for stinky, pigheaded pigs.

Qq is for stinky, quiet quails.

Rr is for stinky, racing raccoons.

Ss is for stinky, STINKY SHOES.

Tt is for stinky, terrible tarantulas.

Uu is for stinky, ugly umbrellas.

Vv is for stinky, vacant vans.

Ww is for stinky, wiggly worms.

Xx is for stinky, Xylo xylophones.

Yy is for stinky, yawning yaks.

Zz is for stinky, zippy zebras.

Activity 2: Practice

Can you read the book, *Stinky ABCs*, again, and write answers on the blank lines below?

Aa is for stinky, _____ _____.

Bb is for stinky, _____ _____.

Cc is for stinky, _____ _____.

Dd is for stinky, _____ _____.

Ee is for stinky, _____ _____.

Ff is for stinky, _____ _____.

Gg is for stinky, _____ _____.

Hh is for stinky, _____ _____.

Ii is for stinky, _____ _____.

Jj is for stinky, _____ _____.

Kk is for stinky, _____ _____.

Ll is for stinky, _____ _____.

Mm is for stinky, _____ _____.

Nn is for stinky _____ _____.

Oo is for stinky, _____ _____.

Pp is for stinky, _____ _____.

Qq is for stinky, _____ _____.

Rr is for stinky, _____ _____.

Ss is for stinky, _____ _____.

Tt is for stinky, _____ _____.

Uu is for stinky, _____ _____.

Vv is for stinky, _____ _____.

Ww is for stinky, _____ _____.

Xx is for stinky, _____ _____.

Yy is for stinky, _____ _____.

Zz is for stinky, _____ _____.

Answer Key for Activity 2

Aa   is for stinky, aging apples.

Bb   is for stinky, babbling bananas.

Cc   is for stinky, choppy cantaloupes.

Dd   is for stinky, dirty dogs.

Ee   is for stinky, eagle's eggs.

Ff   is for stinky, fidgety feet.

Gg   is for stinky, galloping galoshes.

Hh   is for stinky, huge houseflies.

Ii   is for stinky, icky iguanas.

Jj is for stinky, jumping jeans.

Kk is for stinky, king-size keyboards.

Ll is for stinky, lazy lizards.

Mm is for stinky, muddy monkeys.

Nn is for stinky number nine.

Oo is for stinky, orange orangutans.

Pp is for stinky, pigheaded pigs.

Qq is for stinky, quiet quails.

Rr is for stinky, racing raccoons.

Ss is for stinky, STINKY SHOES.

Tt   is for stinky, terrible tarantulas.

Uu   is for stinky, ugly umbrellas.

Vv   is for stinky, vacant vans.

Ww   is for stinky, wiggly worms.

Xx   is for stinky, Xylo xylophones.

Yy   is for stinky, yawning yaks.

Zz   is for stinky, zippy zebras.

About the Author

Debra J. Thomas Mines grew up in Cleveland, Ohio, USA. After graduation from East High School, she attended Ohio Wesleyan University and graduated with a Bachelor of Arts Degree in Elementary Education with a concentration in Reading instruction. Soon after graduation, she married the late Herman C. Mines and enjoyed family life with him and their two children, whom they read to continuously. During these years Debra J. Mines also graduated from Case Western Reserve University with a Master of Arts Degree in Curriculum and Instruction with specialization in Reading Supervision. Additionally, she completed all but the dissertation for a doctorate in Educational Administration from the University of Akron and later achieved the distinction of being a National Board-Certified Teacher (NBCT).

Debra J. Thomas Mines has taught children to read and write from pre-school through eleventh grade. Additional highlights of her career include teaching graduate-level courses as a part-time instructor at Cleveland State University and teaching graduate courses for the Summer Institute for Reading Intervention sponsored by Ohio's Northeast Regional

About the Author continued:

Professional Development Center. Finally, as a professional teacher and life-long learner, she is compelled to learn as much as possible about her students, their cultures, and communities. This desire motivated her to complete programs for the English to Speakers of Other Languages (ESOL) Endorsement and the Gifted In-Field Endorsement. She enjoys teaching diverse populations of students and looks forward to continuing to share her stories, knowledge, and skills to help each child to reach his/her highest potential.

Visit https://www.stinkyshoes.shop to purchase other books written by Debra J Mines.

Made in the USA
Monee, IL
05 September 2022

949e5287-0576-422b-b5af-c45dee94c31eR01